Pure Love

As expounded by the
Gnani Purush Dada Bhagwan

Originally Compiled in Gujarati by :
Dr. Niruben Amin

Publisher : Mr. Ajit C. Patel
          Dada Bhagwan Aradhana Trust
          Dada Darshan, 5, Mamta Park Soc,
          B/h. Navgujrat College, Usmanpura,
          Ahmedabad-380014,
          Gujarat, India.
          Tel. : +91 79 3983 0100

First Edition	: 2000 copies, March 2004
Reprint	: 7000 copies, January 05 to November 2010
New Reprint	: 3000 copies, October 2015

Price   : Ultimate Humility (leads to Universal oneness)
              and Awareness of "I Don't Know Anything"

             Rs. 20.00

Printer   : Amba Offset
            Basement, Parshwanath Chambers,
            Nr. RBI, Usmanpura,
            Ahmedabad-380014, Gujarat, India.
            Tel. : +91 79 27542964

Trimantra
(The Three Mantras)

Namo Arihantanam
I bow to the Lord who has annihilated all the inner enemies of anger, pride, attachment and greed.

Namo Siddhanam
I bow to all the Lord who have attained final liberation.

Namo Aayariyanam
I bow to all the Self-realized masters who unfold the path of liberation.

Namo Uvazzayanam
I bow to the Self-realized teachers of the path of liberation.

Namo Loye Savva Saahunam
I bow to all who have attained the Self and are progressing in this path in the universe.

Eso Pancha Namukkaro
These five salutations.

Saava Paavappanasano
Destroy all the sins.

Mangalanam cha Saavesim
Of all that is auspicious mantras.

Padhamam Havai Mangalam
This is the highest.

ॐ Namo Bhagavate Vasudevaya
I bow to the One who has become the Supreme Lord from a human being.

ॐ Namah Shivaaya
I bow to all auspicious beings of this universe who are the instruments of salvation of the world.

Jai Sat Chit Anand
The Awareness Of The Eternal Is Bliss.

Note About This Translation

The Gnani Purush Ambalal M. Patel, also commonly known as Dadashri or Dada, had said that it would be impossible to translate his satsangs and the knowledge about the Science of Self-Realization verbatim into English because some of the meanings would be lost in the process. Therefore, in order to understand precisely the science of Akram Vignan and Self-Realization He stressed the importance of learning Gujarati.

Dadashri did however grant his blessings to translate his words into English and other languages so that spiritual seekers could benefit to a certain degree and later progress through their own efforts.

This is a humble attempt to present to the world, the essence of His Knowledge. This is not a literal translation but great care has been taken to preserve His original words and the essence of His message. For certain Gujarati words, several English words or even sentences are needed to convey the exact meaning; hence, many Gujarati words have been retained within the English text for better reading flow. At the first encounter, the Gujarati word will be italicized followed by an immediate explanation of its meaning in brackets. Thereafter the Gujarati word will be used in the text that follows. This serves as a two-fold benefit: firstly ease of translation and reading and secondly it will make the reader more familiar with the Gujarati words critical for a deeper understanding of this science. A glossary of all the Gujarati words is provided at the back of the book. For additional glossary, visit our website at :

www.dadabhagwan.org

Many people have worked diligently towards achieving this goal and we thank them all. Please note that any errors encountered in this translation are entirely those of the translators.

* * * * *
4

Books of Akram Vignan of Dada Bhagwan

1. Adjust Everywhere
2. Ahimsa : Non-Violence
3. Anger
4. Aptavani - 1
5. Aptavani - 2
6. Aptavani - 4
7. Aptavani - 5
8. Aptavani - 6
9. Aptavani - 8
10. Aptavani - 9
11. Autobiography of Gnani Purush A.M.Patel
12. Avoid Clashes
13. Brahmacharya : Celibacy Attained With Understanding
14. Death : Before, During & After...
15. Flawless Vision
16. Generation Gap
17. Harmony In Marriage
18. Life Without Conflict
19. Money
20. Noble Use of Money
21. Pratikraman : The master key that resolves all conflicts (Abridge & Big Volume)
22. Pure Love
23. Right Understanding to Help Others
24. Science of Karma
25. Science of Speech
26. Shree Simandhar Swami : The Living God
27. The Essence Of All Religion
28. The Fault Is Of the Sufferer
29. The Guru and The Disciple
30. Tri Mantra : The mantra that removes all worldly obstacles
31. Whatever Happened is Justice
32. Who Am I ?
33. Worries

'Dadavani' Magazine is published Every month

Introduction to The Gnani

One June evening, in 1958 at around six o'clock, Ambalal Muljibhai Patel, a family man, and a contractor by profession, was sitting on a bench on the busy platform number three at Surat's train station. Surat is a city in south Gujarat, a western state in India. What happened within the next forty-eight minutes was phenomenal. Spontaneous Self-Realization occurred within Ambalal M. Patel. During this event, his ego completely melted and from that moment onwards, he became completely detached from all of Ambalal's thoughts, speech, and actions. He became the Lord's living instrument for the salvation of humankind, through the path of knowledge. He called this Lord, 'Dada Bhagwan.' To everyone he met, he would say, "This Lord, Dada Bhagwan is fully manifested within me. He also resides within all living beings. The difference is that within me He is completely expressed and in you, he has yet to manifest."

Who are we? What is God? Who runs this world? What is karma? What is liberation? Etc. All the world's spiritual questions were answered during this event. Thus, nature offered absolute vision to the world through the medium of Shree Ambalal Muljibhai Patel.

Ambalal was born in Tarasali, a suburb of Baroda and was later raised in Bhadran, Gujarat. His wife's name was Hiraba. Although he was a contractor by profession, his life at home and his interactions with everyone around him were exemplary, even prior to his Self-Realization. After becoming Self-Realized and attaining the state of a Gnani, (The Awakened One, Jnani in Hindi), his body became a 'public charitable trust.'

Throughout his entire life, he lived by the principle that there should not be any commerce in religion, and in all commerce, there must be religion. He also never took money from anyone for his own use. He used the profits from his business to take his devotees for pilgrimages to various parts of India.

6

His words became the foundation for the new, direct, and step-less path to Self-Realization called Akram Vignan. Through his divine original scientific experiment (The Gnan Vidhi), he imparted this knowledge to others within two hours. Thousands have received his grace through this process and thousands continue to do so even now. 'Akram' means without steps; an elevator path or a shortcut, whereas 'Kram' means an orderly, step-by-step spiritual path. Akram is now recognized as a direct shortcut to the bliss of the Self.

Who is Dada Bhagwan?

When he explained to others who 'Dada Bhagwan' is, he would say :

"What you see here is not 'Dada Bhagwan'. What you see is 'A. M. Patel.' I am a Gnani Purush and 'He' that is manifested within me, is 'Dada Bhagwan'. He is the Lord within. He is within you and everyone else. He has not yet manifested within you, whereas within me he is fully manifested. I myself am not a Bhagwan. I too bow down to Dada Bhagwan within me."

Current link for attaining the knowledge of Self-Realization (Atma Gnan)

"I am personally going to impart siddhis (special spiritual powers) to a few people. After I leave, will there not be a need for them? People of future generations will need this path, will they not?"

~ **Dadashri**

Param Pujya Dadashri used to go from town to town, and country to country, to give satsang and impart the knowledge of the Self as well as knowledge of harmonious worldly interaction to all who came to see him. During his final days, in the fall of 1987, he gave his blessing to Dr. Niruben Amin and bestowed his special siddhis upon her, to continue his work. "You will have to become a mother to this whole world, Niruben" He told her as he blessed her. There was no doubt in Dadashri's mind that Niruben was destined to be just that. She had served him with utmost devotion day and night for over twenty years.

Dadashri in turn had molded her and prepared her to take on this monumental task.

From the time of Pujya Dadashri's mortal departure on January 2 1988 to her own mortal departure on March 19th 2006, Pujya Niruma as she lovingly came to be called by thousands remained true to her promise to Dadashri to carry on his mission of the world's salvation. She became Dadashri's representative of Akram Vignan and became instrumental in spreading the knowledge of Akram Vignan throughout the world. She also became an exemplary of pure and unconditional love. Thousands of people from all walks of life and from all over the world have attained Self-Realization through her and are established in the experience of the pure Soul, while carrying out their worldly duties and obligations. They experience freedom here and now, while living their daily life.

The link of Akram Gnanis now continues with the current spiritual master Pujya Deepakbhai Desai whom Pujya Dadashri had also graced with special siddhis to continue to teach the world about Atma Gnan and Akram Vignan. He was further molded and trained by Pujya Niruma who blessed him to conduct Gnan Vidhi in 2003. Dadashri had said that Deepakbhai will become the decorum that will add splendor to the Lord's reign. Pujya Deepakbhai, in keeping with Dada's and Niruma's tradition travels extensively within India and abroad, giving satsangs and imparting the knowledge of the Self to all who come seeking.

Powerful words in scriptures help the seeker in increasing his desire for liberation. The knowledge of the Self is the final goal of all one's seeking. Without the knowledge of the Self there is no liberation. This knowledge of the Self (Atma Gnan) does not exist in books. It exists in the heart of a Gnani. Hence, the knowledge of the Self can only be acquired by meeting a Gnani. Through the scientific approach of Akram Vignan, even today one can attain Atma Gnan, but it can only occur by meeting a living Atma Gnani and receiving the Atma Gnan. Only a lit candle can light another candle.

The word love has been misused to such an extent, that every step of the way we question its meaning. If this were real love, then how can it be like this? Where can one find love? What is real love?

Only the Gnani (The Enlightened One) who is the embodiment of love can give us the real definition of love. Real love does not increase or decrease. That which increases or decreases is not love; it is infatuation and attraction (attachment, infatuation or love associated with expectation)! Only love of the Supreme Soul has no expectations or self-interest. It is the love that does not look for faults and never changes. It does not overflow when someone offers praise nor does it turn hostile towards the one who insults. This kind of constant and unlimited love is the incarnate Supreme Soul of the Gnani. Such unparalleled love can only be discerned in the Gnani Purush or a complete Vitarag (one who is free from any attachment) Lord.

People believe that moha (attachment) is love! In moha, there is expectation of reward! If this reward is not received, the person feels dejected! There should be sincerity in love and not close-mindedness. A mother's love is considered the highest in the world, but it too has expectations and disappointments in every corner. It is called infatuation and attraction because there is moha associated with it.

A young man's success at school is celebrated with a party by his parents. They never tire of praising him! They buy him a motorbike and within a few days he wrecks it. The parents get angry and call him all kinds of names and tell him that he does not deserve anything. They take back the 'certificate of merit' they gave him only a few days ago. All their love vanishes! Can this be called love?

In worldly interactions, only love can win over children,

workers and everyone else. Any other means will ultimately prove to be futile.

Even in this time cycle, thousands of people have experienced the supreme love in Pujya Shree Dada Bhagwan. If a person were to experience this love and oneness of being with the Gnani Purush just once, he will constantly meditate on Dada. Dada will always be in his memory, in spite of being bound by life's miseries!

For years now, thousands of people have not been able to forget Dada, even for a second. That is the greatest wonder of our times! Thousands have met him but his compassion and love has been bestowed on them all and they have all experienced it. Each person individually feels that he is favored over others when it comes to being blessed.

One can never find anything comparable to the love of the one who is a complete Vitarag. If one were to behold a Vitarag and experience his aura of detachment (vitaragata) just once in his life, he would surrender himself completely. He will never be able to forget that love for even a moment!

One sees the results and fruits of Dada's compassion, love and his unwavering awareness of how people in this world can achieve salvation.

If one wants to acquire the supreme love, a love that this world has not seen, heard, believed or experienced before, then one should worship the living embodiment of love, the Gnani Purush. How is it possible to put this all in words?

- **Dr. Niruben Amin**

Contents

Pure Love

Love : Real And Relative

Questioner: What is love (prem) in reality? I want to understand it in detail.

Dadashri: When people talk about love in this world, they say it without understanding what it is. Should there not be a definition for love? What is the definition for love?

Questioner: Some call it attachment; some call it affection. There are many kinds of love.

Dadashri: No. There has to be a definition of real love.

Questioner: Can we call it real love when there is no expectation in it?

Dadashri: Love without expectation does not exist in the worldly life. Real love can never be found in this worldly life. Real love is divine. Real love begins the moment one begins to understand one's Real Self (the Soul).

Questioner: What is this worldly thing called love?

Dadashri: The word love belongs to a state, which is beyond the world but it has slipped into the worldly interactions and people's daily lives. In reality people do not understand love at all.

Love Does Not See Faults

Dadashri: Do you have love within you? Do you have love for your children?

Questioner: Yes, I do.

Dadashri: So do you ever hit them or scold them?

Questioner: Surely sometimes we have to scold them.

Dadashri: Love does not see faults. If you see faults in your children, then it is not love. Do you not think so? I have love towards everyone. So far I have not seen a single fault in anyone. So now tell me who do you have love for? You tell me that you have a lot of love within you, so where is this love?

Real Love Has No Motives

Questioner: So only the love for God can be called love?

Dadashri: No. What you have for God is not love. Love is a different thing. There should be no motive behind love. If you have love for God, then why do you not have love for others? You have love for others because you have a need for them. You have love for your mother, because you need her. Love should be without any motive. I have love towards you as well as all these people, but I do not have any motives behind it.

Love Is Not Selfish

The world is very selfish. As long as there is the ego of 'I am', there is selfishness and wherever there is selfishness, there can never be love and wherever there is love, selfishness cannot exist there.

Pure love, real love exists where there is no selfishness; where there are no feelings of 'yours-mine'. Wherever there is a feeling of' 'yours-mine', there is definitely selfishness as well as ignorance of the Self. It is because of this ignorance that people have feelings of 'this is mine and this is yours'. When one acquires Gnan (knowledge of the Self), one ceases to have feelings of 'mine and yours'. However, this is difficult for one to understand.

What people call love in this world, is the language of illusion and deception. The warmth of real love is very different. Love is something very divine.

Prem = A Word Of Two-And--Half Syllable

Saint Kabir had said:

'The world has died studying scriptures,
 not a single learned person has arisen:

The One who understands the two and a half syllable word
Of prem-love, has learnt something indeed.'

Saint Kabir has said that it is enough for one to just understand the word love; one is considered a learned man if he understands this word. People have died studying volumes and volumes of books in an attempt to understand this word and as yet no one has understood it. It is madness to look for its meaning in books.

People would never separate from one another if they had real love. The love they have is selfish, with expectations and motive. How can one call it love?

Questioner: Is it infatuation?

Dadashri: It is infatuation. Real love is the union with the Self, which is free of any attachments. Only the Self is love. Only the knowledge of the Self gives rise to real love.

The Exact Definition Of Love

Dadashri: What is the definition of love?

Questioner: I do not know, Dada. Please explain it to me.

Dadashri: I too was looking for the definition of love when I was young! I wondered about the nature of love. People keep talking about love all the time. What could it be? So then I read all kinds of books and scriptures but did not find the definition of love anywhere. I was astonished that no scripture has defined love. It wasn't until I read a book of Kabir that I was satisfied. He is the one who defined love. His definition helped me. It says:

'That which increases one moment and decreases the next, is not love: That which resides in the heart and remains the same, is real love.'

I found this to be a beautiful definition. 'Bravo! Kabir Sahib, I must say!' This is the truest love of all. That, which never increases or decreases, is love.

Questioner: So what is called real love?

Dadashri: Real love never increases or decreases. The Gnani's love is such a love; it does not increase or decrease. I have that kind of love for the whole world. That love is the Absolute Self.

Questioner: Still there must be love somewhere in this world?

Dadashri: There is no love anywhere. There is no such thing as love in this world. It is all infatuations and attractions. You will realize this right away when someone you love says something negative about you.

If your brother returns home today after being away for a long time, you love to be around him all the time. You will eat together and go out with him. But if the next day he tells you that you are behaving like a person without any sense, this would be the end of your love. If you were to say the same thing to a Gnani Purush several times over, he would not be affected. His love for you would remain the same.

Real love is that which does not have any abhorrence behind it. How can it be called love when there is abhorrence associated with it? Love should be unwavering, unchanging.

Absolute Self Is Love

Questioner: So real love does not increase or decrease.

Dadashri: Real love does not increase or decrease. Love between two people will decrease if one becomes angry with the other and they both start to quarrel. Their love will increase once again, when one gives flowers to the other.

Questioner: In the worldly affairs it is bound to increase and decrease. That is just the way it is.

Dadashri: People's love increases and decreases throughout the day! It fluctuates with their children, their relatives and even for themselves. When they look at themselves in the mirror, they think they look good one moment and the next time they look, they are displeased. All this happens because one does not realize one's own responsibility. How tremendous that responsibility is!

Questioner: That is why people are told, 'love one another, love one another.'

Dadashri: But it is not even love to begin with. Such talks are from the worldly perspective. Who can call this love? The love that increases and decreases is nothing but infatuation and attraction. The world has never seen real love. My love is real love, which is why it affects people. People benefit from it; otherwise it would be of no use to anyone! Whenever there is a presence of the Lord or a Gnani Purush in this world, people witness real love. That love will not increase or decrease. It is love without attachment. It is the love of the Gnani. The Gnani's love is parmatma (absolute Self). Real love is parmatma; nothing else is parmatma.

The Gnani's Love Remains Constant

Questioner: So can you explain the different kinds of love?

Dadashri: There are only two kinds of love: That which increases and decreases, is called attraction and infatuation and the other, which remains constant is love without attachment, attraction or infatuation. This type of love is the love that the Gnani has.

The Gnani's love is pure love. You will not see that kind of love anywhere in this world. The love you see in the world is selfish love. The love between a husband and wife, parents and children and in other relationships is all selfish love. One realizes this when that love fractures, breaks and ends. As long as there is sweetness in it, everything is fine, but one will realize what kind of love it is when it becomes bitter.

For his entire life, a son lives with complete reverence for his father, but if just once, in anger during an argument between the two, the son tells his father, 'you do not have any sense', their relationship is ruined for the rest of their lives. The father will disown the son. Now if it were real love, the relationship would remain unaffected. Selfish love is infatuation and attraction. It is a love like that between a businessman and his customer; it is nothing but transactions of give and take. People are drawn to real love. They are attracted to all the words that flow from real love. There is no action and reaction in real love. The flow of love is constant. His or her love remains constant; there is no increase or decrease, no give or take. Infatuation and attraction is by nature conditional and involves give and take.

My love is constant for everyone at all times. It remains unaffected whether someone insults me or gives me a lot of attention and respect. What people say to me or do for me has no bearing on my love. That is called love. My love for you today will be the same even when we meet after twenty years.

Worldly Love Is Selfish

Questioner: In this world a mother's love is considered very superior.

Dadashri: Then what kind of love comes after that?

Questioner: There is no other. All others types of love have motives and selfishness.

Dadashri: Is that so? Even the love between brothers and sisters is selfish? Have you experienced any of them?

Questioner: I have experienced them all.

Dadashri: When people shed tears, it is not because their love is real. They cry out of selfish motives. The selfishness gives rise to attachment and attraction. Their love arises out of motives and self-interest. At your home you should aim for an unchanging love for everyone. But for the sake of your worldly interactions, you should also tell them: 'I am lost without you, I miss you etc.' You have to say this in order to maintain your relationships. But keep your love such that it does not increase or decrease.

If people ask me, is the love of a woman real love? I would explain to them that the love that increases or decreases is not real love. It is not called love when it increases the day she is given a diamond and decreases when she does not get what she wants.

Questioner: What is real love like when it does not fluctuate?

Dadashri: It does not increase or decrease. It remains the same, whenever you look at it. Elsewhere in the world as long as you do favors for people, their love will stay with you and it will fall apart when you stop. How can you call that love?

So what is the definition of real love? Real love is that which remains the same whether one receives flowers or thorns of insults. This is the definition of real love. Everything else is false attachment and attraction. Real love is the love of the Lord. When that kind of love arises, there is no need for anything else. Only this love is a love that is of any value.

Love Of Illusion Is Useless

Questioner: Can a man live without love?

Dadashri: A man continues to live when the one whom he has loved divorces him, does he not?

Questioner: One can live if it is real love. If it is false love, love of infatuation and attraction, then he will not be able to live with it.

Dadashri: You said it right. Forget about the kind of love, which leads to divorces. How can you call it love? Our love should be such that it never goes away, no matter what happens. One can live with such real love.

Questioner: If it is love of infatuation and attraction, then one cannot live.

Dadashri: The false love of attachment and attraction due to illusion is useless. Do not become trapped by it. Love has to be right and real. It is true that man cannot live without love, but that love has to be real.

So do you understand the definition of love? Look for that kind of love. Do not look for love that ends in a divorce in the future. Where is the stability in such a love?

Questioner: In the worldly love, which is due to attachment, there is expectation of some kind of reward for the sacrifice one makes, whereas in real love there are no expectations of any reward. If one surrenders with unconditional love, does one become divine?

Dadashri: If any man in this world begins on the path of real love, he would become God. Real love is unadulterated and pure. Real love does not have motives of sex, greed or pride. Such unadulterated love turns man into God. The methods are all easy, but to become that is difficult.

Questioner: Likewise if one surrenders to any worldly love and passion what ever it may be, with total devotion and dedication, will it result in attaining the divine state? Will he attain his goal of the absolute in this manner?

Dadashri: If he surrenders to illusion and worldly objects, he will get more of the same, more of the world and increased illusion. That is what has happened to all in the world.

Questioner: These days, boys and girls fall in love because of infatuation and attraction. Do they fail because of this illusionary love?

Dadashri: Yes, it is only because of illusion and infatuation. One sees a beautiful face, and falls in love. But this is not love. Now if there were a boil on that face, one would not even go near her. If the boil were to remain on her face for twelve months or so, he would not want to see her face and his illusion of love disappears altogether. Real love on the other hand, would not disappear even if there were numerous boils. So look for this kind of love, otherwise do not get married at all or else you will be trapped.

A man appreciates his wife when she talks sweetly to him but when she pouts he says he does not like to look at her face.

You foolish man, 'It is precisely because of that sweet face that you were attracted and now you are repulsed by the bitter look on it! This is the same face that you had loved before!'

Questioner: But that is infatuation and attraction, is it not?

Dadashri: All of it is infatuation and attraction. What was 'liked is now repulsive, what was loved is now not loved.' Thus they go on and on. This is how they quarrel. Of what use is this kind of love?

The Illusion And Its Deceit And Pain

If a person has a lot of attachment due to illusion, that attachment will go away if that person experiences a lot of suffering. It was only false attachment, illusion to begin with, and this is the cause of suffering.

Questioner: What is the difference between love of illusion and real love?

Dadashri: The moth hovers around the flame and sacrifices its life in it. That is called love of illusion, whereas real love will last. There is no illusion in real love.

Life of false attachment is useless. It is equivalent to being blind. It is like a blind man who wanders around like the moth and gets consumed in the process. Love on the other hand is constant and it gives lifelong happiness. It does not seek instant gratification.

Therefore, all these are false attachments of illusionary love. Everything is an illusion. Love of illusion is simply open strokes of deceit.

Questioner: But how can an ordinary individual know the difference between real love and false love? How does the other person know whether one's love is real or false?

Dadashri: You will find out when you test it. It is best to test it before committing yourself. Just as we tap a rupee coin to test its authenticity, find an excuse to scold the other person and see their reaction. Nowadays selfishness is rampant. People will feign love for selfish motives. You should test it to see whether it is real love or not.

Questioner: Even when you scold...what is that real love like?

Dadashri: The one with such love will remain calm when scolded and take the utmost care not to hurt the offender. In the presence of such love even the wicked person would melt and surrender.

Real Love Versus An Affair Of Infatuation

Questioner: What kind of love is it when two lovers commit suicide because there is no acceptance from their families?

Dadashri: Aimless, useless love! How can you call that love? They become emotional and lie across the railroad tracks to commit suicide! Then they will say to each other, 'we will be together alone in our next life.' No one should have such expectations. It is each individual's karma that determines where he or she will go. They will never be together.

Questioner: Would they not be together even though that was their wish?

Dadashri: Nothing happens by wishing. The next life is the result of karma of this life. These are all emotional reactions.

Did you have an affair of infatuation when you were young? It is when all the evidences and circumstances come together, that one gets involved in this kind of a problem.

Questioner: What is an affair of infatuation?

Dadashri: Yes, I will tell you. A man had seen his son who was at college, going around with a girl. He asked his son why he was going around in a state of infatuation. People nowadays do not call it so but in the old days they used to call it a lafroo, a temporary state of infatuation and attraction. The father referred to it as lafroo because he knew that his son was being foolish in thinking that he was in love and was going to suffer tremendously from that relationship. This lafroo was clinging to him and it would hurt him. It is not easy to sustain love. Everyone knows how to have love affairs, but they do not know how to break away from such a love.

The son became very upset when he heard his father refer to his girlfriend as a lafroo. He told his father that he was ruining his reputation by saying such things and asked him not to speak in this manner in public. The father agreed. The son dated this girl for two years and then one day he saw her with another boy at the movies. It was then that he realized that his father was right all along. His relationship with the girl was a lafroo.

When all the evidences and circumstances come together, one will become stuck with a lafroo and it will be very difficult to get free from it and when she starts seeing someone else, he will not be able to sleep at night. Does this not happen? From the moment the son realized what his father had said and recognized that it was truly a lafroo, a false love, it began to release him from its grip. As long as he saw her as his girlfriend and not a lafroo, he was bound to her.

Questioner: So if one wants to sum up the differences between false love and real love, how can one do that?

Dadashri: Why are you talking about love when there is no love? Besides real love there is no other love at all; it is all attachment, attraction and illusion. People become blind with illusion and lose sense of reasoning. They have no awareness in this matter.

Real Love Is Sincere

No matter how many terms or conditions of an agreement or promises are broken by the other, the one with real love continues to remain sincere. Such sincerity remains in actions and also in the eyes of the one with real love. That is when you will know that, that is where the real love is. So look for this kind of love. What you see in the world is not real love, nothing but a market place of false love, ordinary love. It is infatuation and attraction and it will bring destruction. Still one does not have a choice, but to go through its trap. Do not despair; I am here to show you real love. One has no choice but fall into the trap of infatuation and attraction.

Attaining The Love Of The Lord

Questioner: So what must one do to acquire the eternal, pure, powerful love of the Lord, the real love?

Dadashri: Do you want to acquire God's love?

Questioner: Yes, I do. Is that not the ultimate goal of every man? My question here is how can one acquire God's love?

Dadashri: Everyone here wants to love, and they would do so if they found sweetness in it!! Show me where people have found such sweetness in God!

Questioner: Even during his final breath, one is not able to call out to God.

Dadashri: How can one take God's name? One can only take the name of that which one has a desire for. One is preoccupied with his desires. His desire is not for God and that is why he is not preoccupied with God. One only remembers God when one is afraid.

Questioner: The desire for God is there, but certain karmic veils of darkness prevent him from taking God's name.

Dadashri: But how can one take God's name without having the love for God? Should not one have love for God? And what is the benefit in having intense love for God? One would love to eat a mango if it was sweet but what if it was bitter or sour? Where have you found such sweetness in God, that you feel love for Him?

God is in every living being, as the Self, the force behind all life, the Soul (Chetan). The world is not aware of the Self, and what it believes to be the Self, is really non-Self. They believe the living body to be the Self, but it is in fact the non-Self. They have absolutely no awareness of the Self. The pure Self is the life force and is the pure Soul (Shuddhatma), and that is God. It is only when we gain some benefit from this God, that we will have love for this God. And as we feel love for Him, we will remember Him and we will utter His name. But first we have to find such a God, only then will we remember Him. Do you remember 'Dada' (The Lord manifest within the Gnani Purush)?

Questioner: Yes.

Dadashri: You think of him because He loves you. He loves you, which is why He remains constantly in your mind. How did this love occur? It occurred because 'Dada' has given you something, a bliss that has blossomed this love. Once this love starts to grow, you will never forget it! You will not have to make an effort to remember Him.

So when do we think of God? It is when He graces us, and gives us eternal bliss, gives us something for which we are eternally grateful. One gentleman told me that he does not like being away from his wife at all. I asked him what would happen to him if his wife were no longer around. He said he would die because she made him very happy. What if she were to abuse him instead of making him happy? Even then he would think of her. Therefore it is because of both the raag (attachment) and dwesh (abhorrence) that people are remembered.

Love Amongst Birds And Animals

One has to understand these things! Right now you wonder whether there is such a thing as love in this world?

Questioner: Nowadays, we think that the affection we have for our children is love.

Dadashri: Is that so? Even a sparrow has love for her young ones. When she returns to her nest with food, the little hatchlings get excited. The sparrow will place one seed at a time in the mouth of each of her young ones. I am amazed as to how she manages to store the seeds in her beak and yet dispense only one seed at a time in the mouths of her hatchlings.

Questioner: But how can they have infatuation and attraction when they do not have any intellect?

Dadashri: Yes. That is what I am telling you. This is just something to illustrate the point. Actually even that is not considered love. Love should be with understanding. Even then it is not considered love. This is just an analogy given to understand the difference between the two. Have you not heard people say that the cow has so much affection towards her calf and she has no expectations in return?

False Love: Infatuation And Attraction Is Associated With Expectations

Infatuation and attraction is found where there is expectation for something in return. How many people must there be in India who have no expectations?

Even when a person grows a mango tree he does it with the expectation that he and his family will enjoy its fruit. He even expects his grandchildren to benefit from it. He does not nurture the tree for the sake of nurturing it and not expecting anything in return. He nurtures it for its fruit. That is why people raise children, for their own benefit, so that their children will take care of them later on. Do you think they raise their children so the children would abuse them when they are old?

Questioner: They raise them so they will take care of them.

Dadashri: But nowadays they abuse them. One man told me, 'My son does not take care of me'. I replied, 'Then what do you expect, you yourself are not deserving of their care.'

Love Of The Mother

Questioner: It has been written in the scriptures that parents have equal love for all their children, is it true?

Dadashri: No. Parents are not God that they can have equal love for each of their children. Only God has equal love for everyone. Parents are just parents, they are not God. They will always be partial. I have equal love for everyone.

The love that people talk about is worldly love. People keep singing about love, but in vain. Even with a woman, how can one have real love? These are all self-serving relationships. And the mothers' love is nothing but the attachment of illusion, because the baby is born from her body. Even the cows have attachment for their offspring, but this attachment lasts only for six months. A mother on the other hand will be attached even when her child is sixty years old.

Questioner: But isn't a mother's love for her child an unselfish love?

Dadashri: A mother's love for her child is not unselfish. This will be evident when the child grows up and one day insults her! During a heated argument, he may refer to her as his 'father's wife'. When the son utters such words, the mother's attachment instantly disappears and she will tell him that she does not want to see his face ever again. Now is not 'his father's wife the same as 'his mother'? But still she will become indignant because he addressed her in this manner. Even she wants reciprocation of her attachment and worldly love. It is all attachment.

So even that love is not unselfish. It is the infatuation and attraction of illusion. Where there is attachment and infatuation and attraction, there is always selfishness.

Questioner: What you are saying is true. As the child grows, the infatuation and attraction increases. But what about when the baby is only six months old?

Dadashri: Even at that time there is infatuation and attraction. The whole day long there is infatuation and attraction. The world is bound through infatuation and attraction. There can never be real love anywhere in this world.

Questioner: I can understand it when you say that about the father, but I still have difficulty accepting it about the mother.

Dadashri: Fathers are selfish whereas mothers are not, when it comes to their children. This is the difference. What does a mother have? All she has is the attachment of infatuation and attraction. They forget everything else and in such situations they can never be without any expectations for even a second. No body can be without expectations. Except for the Gnani, no one can be without any expectations. All these people that claim to be unselfish and without expectations are actually taking advantage of the world.

The Test Of Love

Questioner: So what kind of love do parents have?

Dadashri: If one day you were to insult your parents, they would retaliate. This worldly love is temporary. It may disappear after a few years. Love should be real. Love should not increase or decrease.

Despite this, when a father gets angry with his son, there is no intent to hurt in his anger.

Questioner: Is that real love then?

Dadashri: That can never be real love. If it were real love, then there would be no anger. Nevertheless, there is no intention to hurt behind that anger, and so it cannot be called anger. Anger is defined as that which has intention to hurt.

Of All Worldly Loves, The Love Of The Mother Is The Highest

Real love should not break under any circumstances. So it can only be called love if it never breaks. That is the test of love. However, whatever love there is which is of any worth, it is the love of a mother.

Questioner: You said that mothers have love and not fathers. So would the father not feel bad?

Dadashri: Even then, there is evidence of a mother's love. The mother feels happy when she sees her child. What is the reason behind that? It is because for nine months the child had made the mother's body a dwelling place. The mother feels that she gave birth to the child and the child feels that he was born out of his mother. This is how intense the oneness between the two becomes. Whatever the mother ate, became blood for the child. So this is a kind of love of oneness. Really speaking it is not love. Relatively speaking it is love. So if love is to be found anywhere, it is with the mother. With her you can see some signs of love. However it is a relative love subject to increase and decrease, and has its limitations. It may fracture at any time.

These are all relative relationships, not real. If the father were to die, his son would follow him if it were real love. That is called love but would any son do that?

Questioner: Nobody has done that.

Dadashri: Has there ever been an exception? Has there not been such a case where the son is so overcome with grief over his father's death that he is ready to die along with his father? Has such an event occurred in Mumbai?

Questioner: No.

Dadashri: So what does he do at the crematorium?

Questioner: He cremates his father.

Dadashri: Is that so? Then he must not eat anything after returning home from the cremation, right? He does eat, doesn't he? So this is all superficial. Everyone knows that this is a relative relationship. The one who is gone is gone. After the funeral the rest of the family come home and have a nice meal.

Questioner: So when someone dies and we weep, is it due to our attachment that we cry or is it because we have pure love for him or her?

Dadashri: There is no pure love in this world. The crying is all due to attachment. This world is never without selfish interests, and where there is self-interest, there is attachment. Even a mother has self-interest. People think that their love for their mother is pure, but every mother has self-interest. However her love has been revered because the self-interest is limited. It is still a consequence of attachment of illusion.

Questioner: That is okay but a mother's love can still be unselfish, right?

Dadashri: It is unselfish up to a great extent and that is why a mother's love is called love.

Questioner: But yet you are saying that it is attachment of illusion?

Dadashri: When people ask me whether there is such a thing as love in this world, I tell them that a mother's love is the closest to love in this world. Elsewhere there is no substance to anything. Of all the love there is, a mother's love for her child is worthy of praise, because there is sacrifice in that love.

Questioner: If that is a fact about the mother, then what role does the father have in this love?

Dadashri: A father's love is selfish love. He believes that the son will perpetuate the family name. Only the mother has some element of spontaneous love, natural love. But even she has expectations and assumes that when the son grows up, he will take care of her and it would be enough for her. This expectation is a type of greed. Real love does not have greed or expectations of any kind. Right now you can see the love that I have, but only if you understand it. I do not need anything in this world. Even if you were to give me all the gold in the world I would not have any use for it. I do not have thoughts about women. I am separate form this body. This body is my first neighbor.

Love Remains Within Normal Bounds

A mother is the embodiment of the Goddess of real love, the Divine Mother. The Divine Mother's love is real, and encompasses the highest qualities in the relative world. A living Lord also has such love. Look for such a love from the one people call God. It is with Him that you would experience real love even if you do something wrong. And such a love would remain the same even if you were to offer garlands of flowers. It is love that will not increase or decrease. This is called real love and that real love is the Divine Lord Himself.

This world has not seen love at all. After Lord Mahavir's departure, this world has seen nothing but infatuation and attraction. In the worldly life what people refer to, as love is really infatuation and attraction. It is considered love as long as it remains constant. When it deviates from normality, increases or decreases, that love is considered infatuation and attraction. A mother's love can be called love but when it leaves normality, it is called infatuation and attraction. Otherwise love is the divine Self.

The Love Between Guru And Disciple

All doors open with pure love. What can one not attain with the love of a Guru? The love between a real guru and the disciple is such that the disciple absorbs everything the guru says. Such is the love between them. But nowadays they both quarrel instead.

Once a guru and his disciple were hitting each other and they could be heard by those living downstairs. Someone with me, said, 'let us go up' (to look). I told him that it was wrong to watch. Things like this happen all the time. This is just the way the world is. Do daughters-in-law and mothers-in-law not fight? This is similar! The enmity that was bound in the past life is now surfacing and dissipating. The vengeance was bound in their past lives. If this world were full of love one would not to leave the side of his guru. Even if he had a chance of earning a million rupees, he would forgo it. But here, even when there is nothing for him to earn outside, he still leaves! Why does he go away? It is because he is basically unhappy at home, and he has not found peace.

Not An Owner Of A Wife But A Companion

'I am Chandubhai', is a wrong belief. These are all wrong beliefs. Husbands become domineering because they consider themselves as husbands; owner of the wife. The wives when dominated try to dominate in return and the cycle continues. They should instead think of themselves as companions of their wives. Would there be any problems then?

Questioner: Dada you use a very modern term.

Dadashri: What else? There will be fewer problems this way. The tussle will end. If they lived as companions they would help each other out. Now if one lives with a companion in a single room home, one person would make tea and the other will finish some other task and in this manner the companionship will last.

Questioner: The word companion is also associated with infatuation and attraction, is it not?

Dadashri: There is infatuation and attraction even in that, but that infatuation and attraction is not like that when the terms, husband and wife are used. The terms, husband and wife are filled with heavy infatuation and attraction, but when the word companion is used, the infatuation and attraction diminishes.

'She Is Not Mine...'

An elderly man had lost his wife twenty years ago. His nephew who was sitting near me said, 'shall I make my uncle cry?' I asked, 'How will you do that? He is now so old.' The young man replied, 'Just watch, and see how sensitive this uncle is.' Then the nephew said, 'what a wonderful lady, my aunt was…how kind she was…' Upon hearing this, the old man became tearful and then burst out crying! How crazy people are! Even at the age of sixty he cries! People even cry while watching a movie. If someone dies in the movie, they start crying also.

Questioner: So why can he not be freed from the infatuation and attraction for his dead wife?

Dadashri: One cannot be freed. The problem was created with him believing, 'She is mine, she is mine.' Now by reciting, 'She is not mine, she is not mine,' the attachment will dissolve. The threads that were wound have to be unwound.

Differences In Opinions And Love

Do you have differences of opinion with your wife?

Questioner: How can a couple be called husband and wife without these differences?

Dadashri: Is that so? Is that the rule? Is it written somewhere that they cannot be called husband and wife if there are no differences of opinion between them? Are there not some differences in opinion?

Questioner: Yes.

Dadashri: Then does the husband-wife relationship not keep diminishing with increasing differences of opinions?

Questioner: Love keeps on increasing.

Dadashri: As love increases, does the difference in opinion not decrease?

Questioner: As the differences in opinions increase, and as the quarreling increases, so does love.

Dadashri: Yes. It is not love but infatuation and attraction that increases. This world has not seen love. Love is very different from infatuation and attraction. You can see love as you are talking to me. Even if you were to get angry with me, you would still see that love and realize what love incarnate is. Are you getting anything out of what I am saying?

Questioner: Yes absolutely.

Dadashri: Yes, be warned, otherwise you will find yourself becoming a fool. Can there ever be love in such relationships? How can you expect to see love in others when you do not have it yourself? It is only when you have love within you that you will see it in others. Beware! When you search for real love, know that you will not find it. The so-called love of nowadays is only selfish love. People are taking advantage of each other whenever they can, whether they know it or not. One is enjoying the other without regards for the other, and that is not love; it is exploitation.

Where Is Love In All This?

One will find out about this so-called love between a husband and wife the day the husband does not bring home any money. His wife will be infuriated. She will even say words like, 'Shall I cook your feet in the fire?' Where does all her love go at that time? It was all infatuation and attraction. Love is there as long as there is food and a good home. If the husband then goes on to have an affair, she will threaten to leave him. The poor husband gives in because he feels guilty. What is the point of this kind of love? Somehow one has to get on with life. The husband has to bring home the money and the wife has to prepare the meals. This is how the husband and wife push the cart of their life forward.

Infatuation And Attraction Causes Reaction

Questioner: Why is it that sometimes although we do not want to harbor abhorrence towards others, we still end up doing it?

Dadashri: Whom are you referring to?

Questioner: Sometimes I feel that way about my husband.

Dadashri: That is not called abhorrence. The love of infatuation and attraction is always reactionary. When couples fight, they will avoid each other. After a few days of maintaining a distance, their love grows again. That same love will then cause conflicts and the whole cycle will begin again. Whenever the love becomes excessive, there will be conflicts. When there are conflicts, internally there is love. Conflicts only take place when there is love. Conflicts are the result of worldly love from the previous life, and this love is excessive. Otherwise there will not be any conflict whatsoever! That is the nature of all conflicts.

What do people say? 'Conflict sustains our love.' There is some truth in this. It is not real love that increases but it is infatuation and attraction that increases as a result of these conflicts. Wherever there is less conflict, there is less infatuation and attraction. Any household where conflicts between husband and wife is reduced, consider that there is less infatuation and attraction between them. Is this something that can be understood?

Questioner: Yes and wherever there is excessive infatuation and attraction, there is also a lot of jealousy.

Dadashri: All these problems, including jealousy arise only from infatuation and attraction. When two people fight a lot with each other, realize that there is excessive infatuation and attraction between them. I do not refer to these conflicts as fighting even if they slap each other. I call it parrot-play. It is like when parrots nudge at each other with their beaks but in the end there is no bloodshed. Such is the play of parrots!

When we hear such truth, we laugh at our mistakes and foolishness. It is when one hears such truth that one feels a sense of detachment towards the worldly life, and one begins to question his past mistakes. Alas! Not only has one made mistakes but one has also suffered tremendously.

Where There Are Faults Or Expectations Love Does Not Exist

The world is perplexed because it believes that infatuation and attraction is love. All this is because of a man's need for a woman and a woman's need for a man. When these needs are not met, there are profuse complaints from the inner working components, the mind, chit, intellect and ego. No one belongs to anyone in this world, even for a minute. This has always been the case and it always will be. This would become evident, if a father were to scold his son for an hour. The son would retaliate and even threaten to sue for his share of the inheritance. Only a Gnani Purush loves you unconditionally. He alone is truly yours.

So do not look for love in this world because there is no such thing as love in it. Love cannot be found anywhere except in a Gnani Purush. Everywhere else love disappears and the quarrels start. That is not called love, it is all infatuation and attraction, but people refer to it as love. People are always contradicting themselves! Quarrels cannot be the result of love. Love means you do not see faults in others.

With love one would never see the fault of the wife or the children throughout his life. In love, one never sees any faults at all. Just look at how people find faults with each other. 'You are like that.' 'No, you are like that.' The world has not seen even an iota of love. All this is infatuation and attraction of illusion.

Wherever there is infatuation and attraction, accusations will occur for sure. That is the nature of infatuation and attraction. Accusations like, 'you are like this and you are like that.' And the spouse will retort, 'you are like that, not me.' Infatuation and attraction exists in the world, because of quarrels. Quarrels are vitamins for infatuation and attraction. If there were no quarrels, one could become enlightened.

Love Is With The Enlightened One Only

Nowadays girls only agree to marry after a close scrutiny of their suitors. Does that mean that they do not fight with their husbands? Then how can that be called love? Love lasts forever. Love is unchanging; whenever you see it, it is always the same. One can find comfort and solace in only this kind of love.

You may want to shower her with love, but when you see her sulking and angry, what would you do with your love then? It would be better to throw it down the drain. What good is the love of a person who goes around sulking? What do you think?

Questioner: That is true.

Dadashri: In love there should be no sulking or moodiness. That is the kind of love you will find from me.

One's love should never fluctuate. If your husband is upset with you, your love for him should not change. If a woman is given diamonds, her love increases. All this is infatuation and attraction. The world is run by infatuation and attraction. The only ones who have the license to love are the Gnanis and the fully enlightened Lords. Their love makes people blissful. This love creates a permanent bond between them. Their love is beyond this world. There is no hint of worldly love in it.

Familiarity Breeds Contempt

Human nature is such that wherever there is too much worldly love it turns into dislike and abhorrence. When we become sick, we tire of the ones we love. We tell them to stay away from us or to leave us alone. You should not have any expectations of love from your husband and he is a fool if he expects love from you. Things are fine when our needs are met. Do we try to make a home out of a restaurant? We go there to have a cup of tea, we pay our bill and then we leave! Similarly all we need to do is to get our work done with ease and minimal friction out of that relationship.

In Infatuation of Love All Faults Are Overlooked

When can one say that they have gained from the family members at home? It is when they feel love towards you and they miss you. They look forward to the times with you. People get married but there is no love there. It is only a sexual attraction and need. If it were love, then no matter how many differences they have, their love would not go away. The absence of such a love is called infatuation and attraction. Infatuation and attraction is a waste. Love worth mentioning used to exist in the past. If the husband went abroad for a prolonged period, the wife's chit (inner attentive vision) would remain with her husband her entire life. She would not think about anyone else. Nowadays if the husband does not return within two years the woman will find someone else. How can this be called love? It is all a waste. In love there is surrender and devotion.

Love is a constant internal attraction. It stays on one's mind the whole day. Marriages end up in two ways: either they will thrive or they will end. Love that overflows will subside again. That which overflows is infatuation and attraction, so stay away from love that overflows. The attraction in love should be for the person rather than his or her physical condition. The love should remain the same even if the external body is diseased or is disfigured. When they are newly married the husband caresses his wife's hand, but if she burns that hand in an accident and asks his help in washing and dressing it, he is repulsed. How can there be such repulsion? Where there is love, there is no repulsion and where there is repulsion, there is no love. Even the worldly love should not increase or decrease to this extent. It should be within limits. A Gnani's love is divine love, which never increases or decreases.

Love should exist everywhere. Only love should prevail in the home. Where there is love, one does not see fault in others. When a man acts like a husband, it is egoism, not love. No matter how many mistakes there are, in love one endures them all. Do you understand that?

Questioner: Yes Dada.

Dadashri: So if there is a mistake, you have to let it go for the sake of love. If you love your son, then you cannot look at his mistakes, moreover you have to reassure him that everything is going to be fine. Love endures everything.

This is all infatuation and attraction! One moment the wife will embrace her husband and the next she will criticize him. There is no criticism in love. In love, one cannot look at any faults. In love you do not see faults in a person, ever. Do these people truly have love? Reject such a love.

You will not see real love in this time cycle. You will not see real love. One man told me, 'I love her so much. Even then she insults and rejects me!' I told him that it was not love. No one rejects real love.

The Husband Looks For Sense, The Wife Looks For Wisdom

Real worldly love is when one completely sacrifices and surrenders, without regards to his or her 'safe side' - selfish interest. Nowadays such sacrifice is very rare and difficult.

Questioner: What do you call such a love? Is it love of exclusive devotion?

Dadashri: This is called love in the worldly sense. It is not considered infatuation and attraction and its rewards are great. But people do not sacrifice themselves, this does not happen! People put themselves first and then proceed. How many men or women are there who do not put themselves first?

On the way to the movies they are caught up in the frenzy of infatuation and attraction and on their way home they fight. He would say, 'you have no sense.' She would respond by saying, 'you are not so wise yourself.'

Questioner: Such are the experiences of everyone. No one will admit this but everyone knows that whatever you are saying is true.

Only Love Wins

Questioner: There are lots of responsibilities in life and it is our duty to carry them out. In the process of carrying out these responsibilities, occasionally some harsh words have to be used. Is that considered a sin, demerit karma?

Dadashri: What is the expression on your face when you utter these words? Is it like a beautiful rose? If there is disgust on your face, understand that you have hurt the other person and created demerit karma. You should say what you have to say with calm and poise, without using bitter words. Speak calmly and with understanding and love, using only a few words and one day you will win him over. If you use harsh words, he will become confrontational and you will bind negative karma. The child will also bind negative karma; he will think, 'You can abuse me while I am young, but I will take care of you when I grow up'. So do not do such things. Make him understand instead. Love will win one day. You will not reap its rewards immediately. Continue your love for a month and then see its results.

Questioner: What should we do if he does not understand, even though we try our best to explain things to him?

Dadashri: There is no need to explain. Just love him. But you should also gently try to make him understand. Do we use such bitter language with our neighbors?

Questioner: But one needs to have so much patience.

Dadashri: If a small rock rolls down from a hilltop and hits you, whom do you blame? Would you not just keep quiet when you do not see anyone and realize that it fell by itself? You do not blame the rock. In the same token, when a person insults you, the insult is your past karmic accounts being settled, except in this situation you see the 'doer', but in reality the insults come by themselves, he is merely instrumental in the process. Everything that happens in this world is settlement of past karmic accounts. New karmic accounts are being created as the old ones are being settled. So when you talk to your children, speak to them gently.

Nurture The Plant With Love

Questioner: If someone is doing something wrong and you comment on his negative actions in order to help him but instead the comment hurts him, how can that problem be solved?

Dadashri: There is no problem in cautioning him, but you should know how to do it.

Questioner: How should we tell him?

Dadashri: If you tell your son, 'You are a donkey. You have no sense,' his ego will be hurt. Does he also not have an ego? If your boss were to tell you the same words at work, how would you feel? You cannot use such words. You should know how to caution him.

Questioner: How should we do it?

Dadashri: Sit down with him and tell him gently that civilized and respectable people do not do such things. Talk to him gently and lovingly. But instead what you do is beat him and scold him. How can this be acceptable?

Without love there can be no solutions. Even when you grow a plant, you have to nurture it with love. Merely pouring water over it and shouting at it will not do it. If done with love, if you talk to it with love, it will give you nice big flowers! So imagine how much more it can affect humans!

Questioner: But what do I have to do?

Dadashri: If your telling him does not produce any results, then you should stop. We are being foolish because we do not know how to say things and if so, we should stop. We lose our peace of mind and spoil our life to come. Who would do such a thing?

Not a single person can be improved in this era of the current time cycle. How can a person improve others while he himself is so full of faults? When he himself is full of weaknesses, how can he improve others? To improve others one needs strength. Here only love is needed.

The Power Of Love

Speak in such a manner that the other person's ego does not arise. Whenever you say anything to your child, your voice should not be authoritative.

Questioner: Yes, you had said that we should stop talking before the other person shuts us out.

Dadashri: Yes that is true. You should stop before you get shut out. It is foolishness to persist to the point where he does not heed you anymore. It should not be like that. I have never used an authoritative voice. Only when children are very young can one use authority in their voice. Even in such a situation, I show only love towards them. I win them with love.

Questioner: The power of love is greater than the power of authority, right?

Dadashri: Yes, but you can only love when all your other weaknesses go away. Children have good hearts. You should be kind to them. You can interfere with those who have a lot of intellect but not with those who are sincere and hearty.

When you plant something you have to nurture it and care for it. You cannot keep yelling at it and demand that it better bring forth big flowers. When even a rosebush thrives with love, what about humans? But these parents beat and abuse their own children!

The world always improves through love. There is no other solution for it. If it could improve through fear, intimidation and repression, then these governments would get rid of democracy and imprison whoever breaks the law and hang him.

Questioner: Sometimes even when we explain with love, he still does not understand.

Dadashri: Then in that situation what else would you do, attack and hurt him?

Questioner: I do not know, what should I do?

Dadashri: If you attack and hurt him, he will react in the same manner. That is how fighting starts. One's life becomes full of conflicts.

Questioner: But how can we stay calm in such situations?

I do not know what to do when that happens. What should I do when he does not understand our love?

Dadashri: What can you do? You just have to keep calm. What else can you do to him? Would you hit him instead?

Questioner: But we have not reached the level where we can remain calm and composed.

Dadashri: Then what else will you do? Jump up and down if you want to! Why do you remain calm when a police officer confronts you?

Questioner: Police officers have authority.

Dadashri: Then you should behave in the same way with your children. Let them have the 'authority' over you. If you remain calm with a police officer, why can you not do the same with your children?

Children Are Hungry For Love

At home you should create such an atmosphere of love that your children would hate to leave. When all they see is your love, and nothing but love, you will make an impression on them and they will listen to you. Then they will accept your values.

Why does a child start to cry when you hit him gently? He cries because he feels the pain from the insult and not the physical pain.

The only way to improve this world is through love. What the world considers love is really infatuation and attraction. You love this child, but you get upset with him when he misbehaves. It is because your love is really infatuation and attraction.

The World Improves Through Love

Improvements can be achieved through love. I improve

everyone through love. I talk to them with love, so things do not get ruined; but if there were even the slightest amount of dislike, it would spoil things. Milk can turn sour with the slightest exposure to bad air, even if no yogurt culture is added to it.

With love, one can say anything. What I am telling you is that the whole world is yours if you become the embodiment of love. Wherever there is animosity, slowly change it to love. It is because of animosity that this world appears callous. Here in my presence, love incarnate, everyone is content and in bliss.

How Can There Be Love Where One Demands Appreciation?

You will not see real love in this era of the current time cycle. A man said to me, "I love her so much and yet she insults me!" I told him, "That is not love, no one would insult love!"

Questioner: Is there any expectation in the love that you are talking about?

Dadashri: Expectation? There is no expectation in love. There is equal love towards the alcoholic as well as the one who is sober. There is no expectation in love. Love never expects anything. Love is beyond all relative dualities.

Questioner: Everyone has expectations and want people to have nice words for them. No one likes insults.

Dadashri: If one wishes to be appreciated, it is not love, but infatuation and attraction. It is all an illusion.

People who expect love are foolish. People will only address you with love if your merit karma is unfolding. Relative, worldly love is the result of merit karma. When your demerit karma unfolds, your own brother, will insult and hurt you, even if you have been there at his side during all his troubles. This is all the effect of merit and demerit karma but we blame others for it. It is like blaming the postman for bringing us bad news.

So it is not real love when your merit karma is unfolding. You will find love only in a Gnani Purush; otherwise, there is no such thing as love in this world.

Preserve Your Inner Wealth

People sever their friendships over external problems. When the friendship begins, they display love externally and also feel the same love internally. But when problems arise, their conflicts too will be external and internal. There should be no conflict internally. Although the other person will not be aware of it, one should still have love for him internally. As long as there is internal harmony, one's humanity will not be lost. One loses humanity when one loses internal harmony.

Love Has No Limitations

Do I not have love within me? Are you the only one who has love? Your love is confined to your wife and your children, whereas my love is limitless.

Questioner: Can love be so limited that it becomes exclusive towards only one individual?

Dadashri: Love has no limitations. If it has limits and is confined, then it is called infatuation and attraction. How can it be limited? If four brothers live under one roof along with their wives and children, as long as they all live together, they will say, 'this is our home'. But when they each move away and make their own homes, they will begin to say, 'this is our home and that is yours'. This is how limitation arises. So the love that had developed and encompassed the entire household has narrowed down upon their separation. As a whole group, their love is intact. Where there is real love, there is no limitation, or separation. It is boundless.

Love Versus Attachment Of Illusion

Questioner: So please explain the words love and attachment.

Dadashri: Attachment is relative and changing and love is real and unchanging. Love does not increase or decrease. If it increases or decreases, it is attachment. When relative love becomes excessive, it is called attachment, and one becomes trapped in it. When attachment decreases it turns into abhorrence. That which is attraction and repulsion is not love. What people call love, the Lord calls attraction.

The Illusion Of Attachment And Attraction

Questioner: Why do people have infatuation and attraction for the world?

Dadashri: The whole world is trapped in infatuation and attraction. Until one realizes the Self, one is engulfed in infatuation and attraction. All these ascetics, monks and religious teachers, are all trapped in infatuation and attraction. When their infatuation and attraction towards their wives and children leaves, it is replaced by infatuation and attraction for scriptures, or the infatuation and attraction of 'I am, I am' takes over. There is infatuation and attraction wherever you look.

Infatuation And Attraction Is Not Real Love

My love does not increase or decrease. Your love increases and decreases and that is why it is called infatuation and attraction. Whenever your love fluctuates for those near and dear to you, 'You' (the Self) should just be the Knower of it. From now on your love should not increase or decrease. If the love increases or decreases too much, it is called infatuation and attraction. Infatuation and attraction is always followed by attachment and abhorrence. It is this infatuation and attraction that people refer to as love.

Questioner: Can you explain the difference between infatuation and attraction and love?

Dadashri: Infatuation and attraction is the opposite of love. The love that this world talks about is worldly love, and that is why this world is so complex itself. This worldly love is infatuation and attraction.

The world is immersed in infatuation, attraction and desire, but the One who resides within, the Self is without all these. Where there is infatuation and attraction, there is desire. Desire is always associated with infatuation and attraction. People claim to be free from desire. Even in their devotion to the Lord, they claim that they have no desire. But in reality one can never be free from desire as long as there is infatuation and attraction.

There is infatuation and attraction in everything. It clings even to material things. If one sees a beautiful tea set, they will get pulled towards it, even if there is no life in it! I once visited a carpenter who would not be satisfied until he had inspected a piece of wood five times over! The piece of wood was round and smooth as satin! He had to feel its smoothness over and over again! What an infatuation and attraction over a piece of wood! So infatuation and attraction is not limited to women only. Wherever there is worldly love that clings, it is simply infatuation and attraction.

From Worldly Love To Real Love

Questioner: You explained the subtle nature of infatuation and attraction. Now how can one be free from it?

Dadashri: It is when one realizes, 'I am beyond attraction and attachment', that one becomes liberated. One does not need to remove the infatuation and attraction; one just needs to realize that he is beyond attachment. Infatuation and attraction will never leave any other way. What happens if you eat something sweet and then drink tea?

Questioner: The tea does not taste sweet.

Dadashri: Yes. Similarly after realizing the Self, one will not find the worldly life as sweet; infatuation and attraction will disappear. Having acquired the Self, when one sustains the state of the Self by abiding by my Agnas (Five dictates to follow after Self-realization (Gnan Vidhi) which helps one maintain awareness of one's real Self), this worldly life will not appear as attractive and binding.

Infatuation and attraction cannot be removed even if you want to. Just as you cannot remove the force of magnetism between a magnet and a pin, the infatuation and attraction in humans does not go. Its power and its force can be decreased, but it cannot be eliminated. Infatuation and attraction only go away when one becomes the Self, the one who is never attracted. Otherwise one is always in attraction, infatuation and attached. As long as 'he' is the owner of his name and believes, 'I am Chandulal', he remains attached and bound. He is bound to his name, bound because he is a husband, a father etc.

Questioner: So when one is not affected by circumstances, is that real love and not infatuation?

Dadashri: No, only when the ego ends does one become unattached, the Self. So when both the ego and attachment, 'I' and 'my' go away, then it is called the liberated detached state, the state of the Self. But such a person is very rare.

Questioner: So there should not be any infatuation and attraction in anything we do, we should not let karma bind...

Dadashri: But infatuation and attraction will remain in a person, it is naturally there because the fundamental blunder is not broken. The root cause of his blunder should be destroyed. What is the root cause? It is his belief of 'I am Chandubhai' (believing his relative self to be his real Self).

When someone insults or accuses Chandubhai, he becomes very angry. This is his infatuation, his weakness, and his illusion of attachment.

This wrong belief is the root cause and the biggest blunder. There is no other blunder. The fundamental blunder is that you do not know who you really are and you believe yourself to be that which you are not. Chandubhai is a name given to you for the purpose of identification. People will say, 'This is Chandubhai. He is an income tax officer,' or 'He is this lady's husband' etc. These are all means of identification only. But all these problems have arisen because you do not have the awareness of your real Self.

Questioner: The ultimate problem lies there, does it not?

Dadashri: That is the root cause, and one will find a solution when it is destroyed.

You see things as good and bad because of your intellect. What is the function of the intellect? It always looks for profit and loss, advantages and disadvantages, wherever it goes. Besides this it has no other function. Now you have to get away from this intellect. You should remain as the Self, the unattached. You should become the Self, the One beyond all attachment and abhorrence. The real nature of the Self is that it is above all attachment and abhorrence. You too should become that. All that is needed is to change your nature, come home to your real nature away from your false nature.

How can one become a God when one still has infatuation and attraction? How can there be union between infatuation and attraction and love? How can one be a God when one has anger within?

Whatever element God is made of, you become that element. That, which is eternal, is liberation. That which remains always, that is liberation.

The Way Of The Liberated One : Dadashri

Questioner: Dada, how did you become liberated?

Dadashri: It was "but natural" (Dadashri's own words). I do not know how it all happened!

Questioner: But now you know, don't you? Please show us these steps.

Dadashri: I did not set out to do anything. Nothing happened. What did I set out to do, and what actually happened? I simply set out to make some khir (dessert) but instead ended up with nectar (amrut). All the ingredients from past lives came together. I knew that I had something special within me. I knew that much and because of that I felt a sense of pride and a certain smugness.

Questioner: I thought that if you would describe the process of how you became enlightened then and I would understand that process.

Dadashri: If you take this Gnan, and follow my Agnas, that is enlightenment. After that it does not matter what you eat, drink or wear, as long as you abide by my Agnas, you are absolutely unattached. These Agnas are protection for your unattached state.

The Atomic Science of Attraction And Infatuation

What can this be compared to? It is like the attraction between a magnet and a pin. If you move a magnet around a pin, the pin would move along with it. When we bring the magnet closer to the pin, the pin will stick to it. How does the infatuation and attraction in the pin arise? Similarly in this body too, because of the presence of the electrical body within, there is a property like that of a magnet. The electricity within gives rise to the body's magnetic property, so when the body encounters atoms compatible to its own, attraction occurs, whilst with others, there is no such attraction. This attraction is known as attachment and abhorrence. People will say, 'I am attracted'. If you do not wish it, then why is your body being pulled against your wishes? So who are 'you' in all this?

If you tell your body 'do not to go there', it will still get up and go. That is because the atoms within are being attracted. The body gets pulled away wherever there are compatible atoms. Otherwise why would our body be pulled when we do not wish for it to be? When people's bodies are pulled towards each other, they say they have too much attachment. But if you ask them whether they wish it, they will say that they do not, but even then they are pulled by their attraction. This then, is not attachment (raag), but the property of attraction. But until one has Gnan, one cannot call it an attraction, because one believes that he is the one who is being attracted. If one has this Gnan, when one is the Self, one would know that it is because of the attraction that the body gets pulled and that He does not do anything. He is simply the Knower. So when this body gets attracted, it is this body, which is involved in activity; it is all an attraction of the atoms. It has nothing to do with the Self.

The nature of the mind, body and speech is of attraction and repulsion, and the nature of the Self is not. The body becomes attracted; it is comparable to the force between a magnet and a pin. A magnet will not attract brass. It attracts only iron, so it only attracts atoms compatible to its own. Similarly the atoms in our body are like that of a magnet; they attract those of their own class. Atoms of similar properties are attracted. A woman will get along with an insane daughter-in-law but not with her own sane sister. That is because the atoms do not match.

That is why even towards one's son, there is only

infatuation and attraction. Infatuation and attraction arises from the coming together of compatible atoms. If these atoms do not match exactly, then nothing will happen. So this is all scientific. Infatuation and attraction is the nature of the body. It is the nature of the atoms.

Infatuation and attraction can either be above normal or below normal. Love is within normality; it remains constant without changing. Infatuation and attraction belongs to the inanimate property of the body, the non-Self and not the real Self.

When one finds harmony and oneness in this world, there is a reason behind it. It is because of the properties of the atoms of infatuation and attraction, but one can never tell what will happen at any given moment. As long as there are matching atoms, the attraction will be there and harmony will prevail. But when the atoms do not match, there will be repulsion, which gives rise to hatred. Therefore wherever there is infatuation and attraction, without doubt there is also hatred. In infatuation and attraction there is no awareness of what is beneficial for one, whereas in love complete awareness is there.

This is the science of atoms. The Self has nothing to do with it. But people are under an illusion about the attraction of the atoms. They believe that they have been attracted. The Self never gets attracted.

Illusion Versus Reality

It is because of the attraction like that between the magnet and the pin that you think that you are attracted because of your love. But there is no such thing as love in this attraction.

Questioner: So don't these people know whether it is love or not?

Dadashri: Everyone understands love. Even a two-year-old child will understand what real love is. That is called love. Everything else is infatuation and attraction.

Love is that which does not increase or decrease under any circumstance. All else is an illusion. And such language is also an illusion.

Enmity Is Borne Out Of Attraction And Infatuation

The world has seen everything except love. What the world calls love, is really infatuation and attraction, and it is because of this infatuation and attraction that these problems arise.

People believe that the world is being sustained through love, but that is not so. It has arisen and is being sustained through hate. There is no foundation of love at all. It has arisen on the foundation of hate and vengeance. That is why I tell you to get rid of your hatred and settle all your accounts with equanimity.

The Lord says that internal difficulties that arise out of abhorrence are beneficial. One can never be free of internal difficulties that arise out of worldly love. The whole world is trapped in such difficulties. So do not become too attached to people. Keep your distance. Do not have worldly love for anyone and do not be trapped by his or her worldly love. But you will not be liberated if you spurn someone else's love either. Beware! If you want to be liberated, be thankful to those who oppose and contradict you. Those who shower worldly love on you bind you and those who oppose you, help you towards your final liberation. You have to free yourself from those who shower you with love, but make sure that you do not reject them in the process. It is through rejection of worldly love that this whole world has arisen.

You Are Beyond Worldly Love

The Self is unattached and free, and You are That. It is not something that I have given you. It is actually 'your' own real nature but you may think that Dada has given you this unattached state, and this makes you feel indebted to Dada. There is no need to thank me. Furthermore, if I were to believe that I am benefiting you, then my love will begin to change. I cannot believe that I am obliging you. Therefore, I have to remain in complete understanding and in absolute awareness.

The detached state is your own nature. What do you think? Is it something that I have given you or is it actually your own inherent nature?

Questioner: My own nature!

Dadashri: Yes, say it like that. If you say, "Dada gave me", to everything, then when will it all end?

Questioner: But it was you who made us aware and awakened us, Dada.

Dadashri: Yes, but that is all I did; I awakened you. But when you say, 'Dada has given me everything', all I have really done is given you what was already yours.

Questioner: You gave us what was ours, but did we even know that it was ours?

Dadashri: You did not know that but you did find out eventually! The glory of this knowing is something else! How glorious this is! This grandeur would not go away even if someone were to insult you. If on the other hand, this knowledge were not there, a person would feel insulted if someone did not acknowledge him in a public reception. Now look at the difference between the two!

Questioner: Wherever we were once attracted, will that all become detached?

Dadashri: Yes, that is the way! These are all the steps. Eventually one has to come to the state of the unattached, the Self.

Intellect Ends Where Love Is

What is God like? He is unattached. He is never attached.

Questioner: Even the Gnani is unattached?

Dadashri: Yes. That is why our love is constant and the same everywhere. It is equal for everyone. My love is the same for those who insult me and for those who shower me with flowers. There is no discrimination in my love and where the love is not discriminating, the intellect disappears. Love destroys intellect or else the intellect will end love. Where there is intellect, there is no love and where there is love, there is no intellect. When intellect disappears, the ego disappears. It is when nothing remains and all attachment is gone, that one becomes the embodiment of love, love incarnate. I have eternal love. I do not have any attachment for this body. I have no attachment for this speech. I have no attachment to this mind.

Love Arises From Absolute Detachment

Real love arises only when the ego and attachment are gone. Real love is something that is born out of absolute non-attachment (vitaragata). First, one has to become free from all dualities, only then one becomes a vitarag. Both duality (dvaita) and non-duality (advaita) are in itself a duality. Those who follow non-duality will have issues about duality. In rejecting duality, they become absorbed by duality. Nevertheless non-duality is of some benefit. It is when one goes way beyond non-duality that one will arrive at the stage of the vitarag, the absolutely enlightened One. The distance between non-duality, advaita and the vitarag is a hundred thousand miles of spiritual travel. And it is here that real love arises. And this love is the Supreme love. Such a love will not decrease, even if someone was to slap him, and if it does decrease, then it was not real love.

It is okay if someone hurts us, but we have to be careful that we do not hurt anyone. Only then can love flow and be experienced by others. Gradually one has to become the embodiment of pure love for everyone.

Questioner: What does it mean to become the embodiment of pure love?

Dadashri: If a person leaves after insulting you, and returns a few minutes later, if your love for him does not diminish, that is pure love (shuddha prem). One needs to learn to have this kind of love, nothing else. You should have the kind of love that I show you. Will you be able to manage this before this life comes to an end? So now learn to have such a love.

The Way To Become The Embodiment Of Love

If one understands the world exactly as it is, and then experiences it from that perspective, then he will become the embodiment of love. What does 'as it is' mean? It means that all living beings are innocent. They are flawless. It is because of illusion that one sees faults in others.

It is an illusion if people appear good and it is also an illusion if they appear to have faults. The former is because of attachment and the latter because of detachment. In reality everyone is faultless. When you see faults in them, you cannot love them. So when you see the world as faultless, that is when pure love will arise. As long as we look upon others as being separate from ourselves, we feel a sense of 'mine' and 'yours'. As long as you keep differences with the other person, you will have attachment towards your own. Those for whom we have attachment, we consider 'ours' and those with whom we feel detachment, we consider as belonging to others. A person with this kind of discrimination can never become an embodiment of love.

The nature of the Self is love and with such a love, one forgets all one's problems. Once bound through this love, nothing else can bind you.

When does love arise? It is when you ask for forgiveness for all mistakes that have occurred so far. You accept that you, and only you are at fault for seeing fault in others. You should take this approach with those for whom you wish to become the embodiment of love. Only then will you feel love. Do you want to love or not?

Questioner: Yes, Dada.

Dadashri: These are all my methods. The very method that guided me to full enlightenment is the same method by which I guide you all.

When you become the embodiment of love, others will experience oneness with you. Everyone has attained oneness with me in this manner. This method is being opened up to everyone.

The One Who Sees 'I' In Everyone Is Love Incarnate

Pure love will increase in proportion to the decrease in differences experienced. What do we need to get rid of in order to develop pure love? One has to be rid of their differences so that pure love can arise. When the differences disappear completely, absolute, pure love is established. This is the only way.

Did you understand this 'point of view'? This is something very different. One has to become the personification of love. One will then feel a sense of oneness with everyone. There will be no discrimination or difference. People usually say, 'this is mine and that is yours!' It is like a disease. Differences exist because of this disease. But when people depart from this world, is there any such thing as 'mine' and 'yours'? Once this 'disease' is eradicated, one will become a personification of love.

Love is when one perceives the Self in all living beings. All this is 'I', and 'I' am in all. Otherwise one will have to say, 'you'. If you do not see, 'I' then you will see, 'you'. Then there will always be a difference between you and others. For worldly interactions, you will have to say, 'I' and 'you,' but in reality you should see 'I' everywhere. To become the embodiment of love is to see everything with oneness, and act with oneness. Get rid of your belief that others are different. You should feel as though everyone is a part of one big family.

The Non-discriminating Love Of The Gnani

Love is when there is no falling apart, no separation. It is called love when there is no discrimination. Such love is said to be within normal limits. If there is any difference in one's love for another person, then it will fluctuate. It will increase when the other person does something good and decrease when he or she does something wrong. It deviates from normality. The real love does not take account of the other person's actions. It only looks at the Self within that person.

Questioner: What is that we feel for you, Dada?

Dadashri: It is my love that grabs you. Real love touches the whole world. Where can you find love? Love is found wherever there is oneness. So when can one attain oneness with the world? It is when one becomes the embodiment of love that oneness with the whole world is attained. There you see only love.

When is it called infatuation and attraction? It is when you want worldly things. When you desire material things. There is no problem with yearning for real happiness. There is no problem with the love you have for me. That love will help you. All other types of love will disappear.

Questioner: So the feelings that we have for you, is it the result of love in your heart?

Dadashri: Yes, it is the result of love. People become wise with this weapon of love. I do not have to scold them.

I do not mean to scold anyone. The only weapon I have is this love. 'I mean to conquer this world with love'.

I have laid down my arms. I have laid down my weapons of anger, pride, attachment and greed. The world wields these weapons of anger, pride, attachment and greed. I aim to conquer the world through love. The love that people know and understand is the mundane worldly love. Real love is that which will not depress me if you insult me, or elevate me if you praise me. In real love no changes occur. If any changes do occur, they will be of this body and not of the pure love. I, the love incarnate, am separate from these thoughts, speech and acts.

Even an attractive person appears ugly because of his ego. When he becomes the pure Self, he will be beautiful. Then even the ugly will look beautiful, but it is only when pure love arises within. People want unconditional love, love devoid of selfishness.

This is nature's law, because love is the Self.

Where There Is Love, There Is Liberation

Where there is no love, there is no path to liberation. Even when one does not know the right things to say, one is offered only love. This is pure love.

God exists where there is honesty in relative interactions and where there is pure love, which does not increase, or decrease. These are the two places where God resides. Where there is love, faith and purity, that is where God is.

Love arises after one transcends the 'relative self' and becomes absolutely independent. Where can one find Gnan, real knowledge? It is where work is achieved through love. There, there is no give or take. There is oneness there. Where there is an exchange of money, there is no love. Do people not charge a fee for their spiritual discourses? That is a business and you will not find love there. Where there is love there is no deceit. Where there is deceit there is no love.

One gets used to wherever one sleeps on, if one sleeps on a mat he gets used to that mat and if one sleeps on a Dunlop mattress, he will get used to that too. If you ask the one who insists upon sleeping on the mat, to sleep on the Dunlop mattress, he would not be able to sleep. Insistence is poison and the absence of insistence is nectar. Until one attains the state where one becomes free of all insistence, the love of the world will not be acquired. Pure love is born out of non-insistence and pure love is the Supreme Lord.

One becomes an embodiment of love when one does not look for rules and regulations. If you look for rules and regulations, you cannot become the embodiment of love. Love is not to be found with the one who asks, 'why are you late?' When you are the embodiment of love, people listen to you. If you have infatuation and attraction, who would listen to you? You need money, you need other women, is that not infatuation and attraction? Even the need to have disciples is infatuation and attraction.

There Is No Emotion In Love

Questioner: It is said that real love arises from the heart. Emotions also arise from the heart, do they not?

Dadashri: No. That is not love. Love is pure. What would happen to the passengers in a train, if the train were to become 'emotional'?

Questioner: There would be a problem. There would be an accident.

Dadashri: People would die. Similarly, when a person becomes emotional, innumerable organisms die within that person's body. He becomes responsible for it. There are many such responsibilities that arise when one becomes emotional in this manner.

Questioner: Without emotion, would a person not become like a rock?

Dadashri: I am 'emotionless'; do I look like a rock? I do not have any 'emotions' at all. One with 'emotions' (above and below normal) becomes 'mechanical' (the non-Self) but one who is 'in motion' (normality) will not become 'mechanical' (remains as the Self).

Questioner: But if a person, who has not attained Self-realization, were to be without 'emotions', would he not appear like a rock?

Dadashri: That cannot happen! It can never happen. Otherwise people will become insane. Even the insane are emotional. The whole world is emotional.

Tears Do Not Express Real feelings

Questioner: You have to express feelings to live in this world. You have to display feelings. If you do not show any feelings, then people will think you are insensitive. Now along with receiving this Gnan, comes the understanding of the Gnan. Then our feelings are not so easily expressed. Should they not be expressed in our daily life?

Dadashri: You just have to observe what happens.

Questioner: Say for example if the son is going abroad for his education and the parents go to see him off at the airport. The mother starts to cry but not the father. People will say that he has no feelings, he is like a stone.

Dadashri: No. His feelings are not like that. So what if the son is going abroad? If she is overcome with tears and starts to cry, you should gently say, 'how long are you going to remain weak like this, especially when you want liberation from all worldly entanglements?'

Questioner: No, if he did not express that much feeling, then a man is considered hard-hearted. A man without feelings is hard-hearted.

Dadashri: True feelings lie with those who do not shed tears. Your feelings are wrong. Your feelings are demonstrated, while his, which are not shown, are real. Feelings are from the heart. People have misunderstood all this. Feelings cannot be forced. It is a natural gift. If you tell someone that he is as hard as a rock, then you will stop whatever feelings he may otherwise have. It is not feelings when one cries one moment and forgets the next. Feeling is not to cry and yet to remember all the time.

Even I have feelings. I never cry and yet I have constant feelings towards everyone. That is because the more the people come to see me, the more they come into my Gnan daily.

Questioner: At times the way the parents show feelings for their children appears to be excessive.

Dadashri: That is all emotional, above or below normality. Even those who show no feelings are considered 'emotional'. It should be within normality. Normal means only dramatic. Just as the actor acts realistically in a play, you should perform your role in life with the same degree of conviction. Even the audiences of the play become convinced that there were no flaws in his acting. The feelings displayed were all for the sake of the play. Do you understand?

Questioner: Yes, I do understand.

Dadashri: So say to your son, 'son come here and sit with me. Besides you, I do not have anyone else'. I too used to tell Hiraba (Dadashri's wife) that, 'when I go out of town, I miss you. I do not like being away from you.'

Questioner: Hiraba would even believe that.

Dadashri: Yes. It is the truth. But internally I did not let it touch me.

Questioner: In the old days parents did not have time to love or attend to their children, and they did not give any love either. They did not give too much attention to their children. Nowadays parents give a lot of attention to their children. They pay a lot of attention to them and yet why is it that the children do not have love for their parents?

Dadashri: This current love is nothing but increasing infatuation and attraction, an illusion of increasing attachment. This results in increased preoccupation with that which attracts them, the children. In the past there was very little attachment, whereas nowadays there is much more attachment to many more objects in the world.

Questioner: Yes, and the parents too, yearn for love from their children. They expect to be respected by their children.

Dadashri: It is love only. The world is dependent upon love. It is not as dependent on material comforts as it is on love. Alas! This love is involved in conflicts. Love should not end up in conflicts.

Questioner: Children also have a lot of love for their parents.

Dadashri: The children too have a lot! But even their love is associated with conflicts.

As Long As There Is Attraction There Is Tension

Questioner: It is believed that where there are more feelings, there is more love.

Dadashri: There is no love there at all! It is all infatuation and attraction. There is no such word as love in this world. To even utter the word 'love' is wrong. It is all infatuation and attraction from within.

Questioner: Then what are all these feelings and sentiments? Can you please explain?

Dadashri: All this sentimental behavior falls under 'emotions'. When a person does not remain 'in motion' (the Self), he becomes 'emotional'.

Questioner: In the English language there are two words-'feelings' and 'emotions'.

Dadashri: Yes, but 'feelings' and 'emotions' are two different things. Sentiments and sentimentality fall under the 'emotional' because they cross the boundaries of normality.

As long as there is any degree of sentimentality, and as

long as there is infatuation and attraction, the person will have tension and it will show on his face. I have love, which is why I live without any tension. No one else can live without tension. Everyone has tension. This whole world has tension!

Gnani Is The River Of Feelings

The Gnani Purush has feelings but they do not touch him internally. He remains as He is, separate and natural. There is no rule that requires that the feelings be felt internally and touch the Self. How can a person be called a human being if he has no feelings?

Questioner: You said that even you have feelings. You have also said that your feelings are like ours, but are higher than ours, because they are for everyone.

Dadashri: Yes I have feelings. I can never be without feelings.

Questioner: And yet these feelings do not 'touch' you?

Dadashri: Yes, I allow these feelings to sit where they belong naturally, in the non-Self, the foreign department. Whereas you make the mistake of letting them sit in a place, which is not natural for it, the realm of the self.

Questioner: Please clarify that demarcation.

Dadashri: One needs to keep separate the foreign (non-Self) and the home (Self). Keep that which belongs to the foreign department in the foreign department, do not bring it home. Whatever goes on in the foreign department, the non-Self should not be allowed to touch the home, the Self. Enter the home after leaving everything in the foreign department.

Questioner: But under the force of the feelings it is difficult to maintain this separation between foreign and home.

Dadashri: Why would it not remain separate for the ones who have taken Gnan? And if I do not get it done, the work is done.

Questioner: I want to understand how you apply that.

Dadashri: I leave the feeling in the foreign department and then enter the home department. If the feeling tries to enter I say, 'sit outside'. Whereas you folks say, 'come on in my dear, welcome'.

The Results Of The Detached State

People tell me that I worry about them. That is true but they do not realize that I do not allow those worries to touch or affect me. Worries can debilitate a person; take away his energies, whereas one can do anything if he does not have worries. Worries can destroy a man. So I do everything superficially and do not allow worries to touch me.

Questioner: So really, you would not do anything. If a Mahatma were suffering deeply, would you not do anything?

Dadashri: Of course I would! But it would be superficial. By superficial I mean that all the work is being taken care of but it is taking place in the foreign department. I would not let it affect me. Everything that the relative-self needs to do should be done. One should let all the external processes take place, but without any worries. On the contrary, things become ruined by worries. Are you really asking me to worry?

When you let something affect you, you become involved and the separation of the foreign and home department gets blurred, and you will not accomplish what you set out to do. This is how everyone in this world reacts and that is why nothing is achieved in this world. When I do not let it affect me, it is a protection for the other person and for me also. This is what I mean by the term 'safe-side'.

I have experienced that the outcome is not good when I

let it affect me. I lose my energies and the other person's work does not get done. And if I do not let it affect me, then the strength of the Self, energies increase and the other person's work is done.

This science is love itself. There is no anger, pride, attachment and greed in love. If any of these exist then it is not love.

Pure Love Is Above Virtuous Love

Questioner: Everyone in the world is searching for pure love but in vain.

Dadashri: This is the path of pure love. This science of ours is void of desires of any kind. This is the path of pure love. Such a path cannot be found in this era of this time cycle and it is indeed a wonder that it has arisen.

Questioner: Can you explain the difference between pure love and virtuous love?

Dadashri: There is ego involved in virtuous love, whereas in pure love, there is no ego. In virtuous love there is no greed or deceit, but there is pride in it. In virtuous love, one has a sense of being: 'I am'. And in pure love, one feels oneness with everyone, because there is no ego.

Questioner: But is it true that in any activity, good or bad, there is no element of ego. Is it logical?

Dadashri: No. That cannot be. That is wrong, because no activity can be carried out without the ego. Even virtuous activities require the ego.

Questioner: Even for pure love ego is necessary. So how can one do so without the ego? Can the ego and pure love co-exist?

Dadashri: As long as the ego is present, there can never be pure love. Ego and pure love cannot co-exist. When does pure love occur? It is when the ego starts to dissolve and only when the ego completely disappears, that one becomes an embodiment of pure love. The embodiment of pure love is the absolute Self. In the presence of the Absolute Self, The Gnani, one can receive all kinds of blessings. The Absolute Self is impartial. It is beyond the scriptures. All the four Vedas say, 'this is not that'. It is the Gnani Purush that says, 'this is that!' The Gnani Purush is pure love and he can give you your Self right away.

Love Illuminates The Divinity Of The Self

Compassion is a universal intent that is felt everywhere in this world. It arises out of one's concern for everyone trapped in the world's miseries and how people's miseries can be alleviated.

Questioner: I want to know the relationship between love and compassion.

Dadashri: Love and compassion are different. Compassion means a generalized awareness of suffering of the entire humanity. This is a type of grace. Love is different. Love is the vitamin for the Self. People have taken a lot of vitamins for the body, but they have never taken the vitamin for the Self. When one sees pure love, the vitamin, the inner energy of the Self expresses.

Questioner: Does it not happen naturally Dada?

Dadashri: Naturally.

Questioner: So there is nothing left for the other person to do?

Dadashri: Nothing at all. This whole path is natural and spontaneous.

Love For The One Who Throws Stones

Questioner: After the Gnan we experience the flow of love, nothing but love. What is that?

Dadashri: That is real attachment (prashasta raag). The attachment with which all other attachments of the world disappear, is what the Lord calls prashasta raag. This attachment is the primary cause for final liberation. This attachment does not bind you because there are no worldly intentions in it. The attachment you feel towards a benevolent One is real attachment, and it is this attachment that will break all other attachments.

When you meditate on Dada, the attributes of Dada will manifest within you. You should not have desire for any worldly things. Just desire the continued bliss of the Self. And if someone were to insult you, your love for him should remain unaffected. As long as you stay this way, your work is done.

The Gnani Purush: Love Incarnate

Questioner: Sometimes during sleep, in a state of light sleep, Dada comes to mind and continues to remain there. What is all that?

Dadashri: Yes. That happens. It is because Dada travels throughout the world in a very subtle form. On a gross level I am here, but 'Dada' in a subtle form roams throughout the world, He watches over everything. He does not bother anyone.

A lot of people have dreams of Dada and sometimes they also converse with Him. Even during the daytime, when they are awake, they talk to Dada. They even write down their conversations and read them to me when they meet me.

Such things continue to happen. There are no miracles in

this. This is natural. Any person that has become free from all the veils of ignorance, but has not yet reached the stage of absolute Knowledge, such a person is the manifestation of real love, and in the presence of such a person, everything is possible.

There are some people, who love unselfishly, but they have egos and so their love is not completely unselfish. Only when their egos disappear, will they have pure love. The Gnani is love incarnate. Whenever a person falls into difficulties, the Gnani is his solace.

Equal Love For All

This love is Godly love! It is not found everywhere! It is very rare.

The Gnani has equal love for everyone, regardless of his or her physical appearance. He loves the fat and the thin, the black and the white, the physically fit and the disabled. Everywhere his love is constant. He does not look at the external but at the Self within and that is why he has equal love for everyone. Just as in the worldly dealings, people do not look at a person's outer clothes but at his human qualities, the Gnani looks at only the Self and not the physical packing.

Such a love attracts everyone, the learned as well as the illiterate, the young and the old. Such a love accommodates everyone. It even attracts the children who come and sit here and do not want to leave because the atmosphere is so beautiful.

Love Of The Gnani

Only the love of the Gnani Purush is worth observing! Today there are some fifty thousand people here, and all feel his love equally. All of them are living with that love.

Questioner: That is very difficult!

Dadashri: But that love has manifest within me. So many people live solely on this love of mine. They are constantly with 'Dada, nothing but Dada'. They are not bothered even if they get nothing to eat. Love is such a thing.

Their sins are completely destroyed with this very love. Otherwise how else were they going to wash away their sins in this era of the current time cycle?

Love Of The Gnani Purush : Love Of The Tirthankar

The world has never before seen the love that is manifest here. Whenever such a love did manifest, it was within the Vitarag Lords and so that love was not visible. In my case because I fell short of achieving Keval Gnan (absolute Knowledge), that love expressed visibly.

Questioner: You said that you became the embodiment of love but an absolute enlightenment, absolute vitarag state did not manifest, can you explain that?

Dadashri: Love is when one does not feel even the slightest of negativity towards anyone. So only absolute vitarag state is called love.

Questioner: Then where is this love located? In what condition is it called love?

Dadashri: As one becomes more and more detached (Vitarag), one's love will arise proportionately. The Absolute Vitarag has absolute love! You have all become vitdwesh (without abhorrence). Now you have to slowly become Vitarag (without attachments) in all matters. That is how love will arise towards the full phase (the Absolute state).

Questioner: Here you have said that you have love, what does it mean when you say that you did not get reach the vitarag state?

Dadashri: Vitarag state is this love of mine. You are able to see my love, but the love of the Absolute Vitarag is not visible. Their love however is considered real love. People can see my love, but that is not called real love. Real love is when one becomes an Absolute Vitarag; complete full moon, whereas for me it is not considered the full moon but the moon of the night before the full moon.

Questioner: That means the love of the one with the full moon is greater than yours?

Dadashri: Yes, theirs is the real love! Real love is of those with the full moon. My love lacks in some places.

Questioner: Can one have absolute vitarag state and yet be lacking in love?

Dadashri: They can never be without love, full love.

Questioner: Is there so much of a difference between the fourteenth day of the moon and the full moon?

Dadashri: Quite a lot of difference! It would appear to be very much like the full moon, but there is a vast difference! What do I have? I have nothing, whereas the Tirthankars, have everything. Nevertheless, the satisfaction I feel is the same as that of the full moon! My energies and powers are such that I feel as if I have achieved the full moon too!!

The Gnani Is Bound By Love

Questioner: Now after taking this Gnan, two to three more lives - births still remain. So are you not bound to help us with your total compassion until they are completed?

Dadashri: I am bound only by love. I am bound as long as there is your love. When your love ceases, then I am free. If your love turns towards the worldly things, then you will not remain bound to me. If your love remains towards the Self, then

I will remain bound to you. What do you think? Are we not bound? We are bound for sure through love!

Pure Love Incarnate Is The Lord

It does not take long to please the one with an ego. He would be very happy even if you were to give him the slightest compliment. A Gnani on the other hand is not easy to please. There is nothing in this world that makes the Gnani happy! Only your love makes him happy, because he is the only one with real love. The Gnani has nothing to offer you but love. He has love towards the whole world.

The pure love that you see of the Gnani Purush, the love that you see clearly, is itself the Divine Lord in human form. The pure love that you can see, the one that neither increases nor decreases, the love that remains constant, is the Absolute Self. The Lord in human form is clearly visible through His love. Gnan is the invisible, subtle form of the Lord, which takes some time to understand. So there is no need to look for pure love outside in the world. Outside, all you have is infatuation and attraction. The love that does not increase or decrease is the divine pure love of The Lord.

Jai Sat Chit Anand

Namaskar Vidhi
The Vidhi of Salutations

- With the live presence of Dada Bhagwan as my witness, with the utmost reverence and devotion, I bow to Tirthankara Lord Shri Simandhar Swami, who at present moves about in Mahavideh world. (40)

- With the live presence of Dada Bhagwan as my witness, with utmost reverence and devotion, I bow to the Om Parameshti Bhagwants, who at present move about in Mahavideh and other worlds. (5)

- With the live presence of Dada Bhagwan as my witness, with utmost reverence and devotion, I bow to the Panch Parameshti Bhagwants, who at present move about in Mahavideh and other worlds. (5)

- With the live presence of Dada Bhagwan as my witness, with utmost reverence and devotion, I bow to all the Tirthankara Lords who currently moving about in Mahavideh and other worlds. (5)

- With utmost reverence and devotion, I bow to all the celestial Gods and Goddesses who protect the sovereign authority of the fully enlightened Lords. (5)

- With utmost reverence and devotion, I bow to the celestial Gods and Goddesses who protect without partiality. (5)

- With utmost reverence and devotion, I bow to the twenty-four Tirthankara Lords. (5)

- With utmost reverence and devotion, I bow to Lord Shri Krishna. (5)

- With utmost reverence and devotion and with full affirmation, I bow to the fully enlightened Shri Dada Bhagwan who is currently moving about in our world.(5)

- With utmost reverence and devotion, I bow to the future Tirthankaras of Dada Bhagwan. (5)

- With utmost reverence and devotion, I bow to all the Self-realized beings of Dada Bhagwan. (5)
- With utmost reverence and devotion, I bow to the real Self in all living beings of this universe. (5)
- The real Self within all living beings is divine, and therefore I see the divine Self in all living beings. (5)
- The real Self within all beings is the pure Soul, and therefore I see the pure Soul in all living beings in the world. (5)
- The real nature of all is eternal and elemental, and with this knowledge of eternal elements I see the entire world. (5)

Nav Kalamo
Nine Deep Inner Intents

1. Dearest Dada Bhagwan, give me the infinite inner energy to not hurt, cause someone to hurt, nor instigate anyone to hurt the ego of any living being, even to the slightest extent. Give me the infinite inner energy not to hurt the ego of any living being and to conduct my thoughts, speech and action in a manner that is accepted by all.

2. Dearest Dada Bhagwan, give me the infinite inner energy not to hurt, cause someone to hurt, nor instigate anyone to hurt the foundation of any religion, even to the slightest extent. Give me the infinite inner energy not to hurt, even to the slightest extent, the foundation of any religion and to conduct my thoughts, speech and action in a manner that is accepted by all.

3. Dearest Dada Bhagwan, give me the infinite inner energy not to criticize, offend, or insult any living monk, nun, preacher or religious head.

4. Dearest Dada Bhagwan, give me the infinite inner energy not to, nor cause anyone to, nor instigate anyone to dislike or hate any living being, even to the slightest extent.

5. Dearest Dada Bhagwan, give me the infinite inner energy not to, nor cause anyone to, nor instigate any one to speak any

harsh or hurtful language towards any living being, even to the slightest extent. If someone speaks in harsh or hurtful language, please give me the strength to speak kindly and softly in reply.

6. Dearest Dada Bhagwan, give me the infinite inner energy not to have, nor cause anyone to have, nor instigate anyone to have any sexual inclinations, feelings or gestures towards any living being, be it male or female or of bisexual orientation.- Give me the supreme energy to be eternally free from all sexual inclinations.

7. Dearest Dada Bhagwan,give me the infinite inner energy not to have any greed towards any taste in food. Give me the energy to take balanced meal consiting of all tastes.

8. Dearest Dada Bhagwan, give me the infinite inner energy not to, nor cause anyone to, nor instigate anyone to criticize, offend or insult any being, present or absent, living or dead.

9. Dearest Dada Bhagwan, give me the infinite inner energy to become an instrument in the path of salvation for the world.

[Dada Bhagwan is The Lord within all living beings. This recitation is meant to take hold within you, and is not to be recited mechanically. Reciting this daily is worthy of your deep inner intent, as this teaching encompasses the essence of all religions.]

Pratikraman : Process of Divine Apology

With Dada Bhagwan as my witness, I offer my salutations to the Pure Soul who is totally separate from the mind, speech and body of * _____

I recall my mistakes (aalochana) **

I apologize for these mistakes (pratikraman)

I affirm not to repeat these mistakes again (Pratyakhyaan)

Dearest Dada Bhagwan ! Grant me the strength to act in accordance with this firm resolution.

* Name of the person hurt by you.

** Recall the mistakes you committed with this person.

Persons to Contact

Dada Bhagwan Parivar

Adalaj : **Trimandir**, Simandhar City, Ahmedabad-Kalol Highway, Adalaj, Dist.: Gandhinagar - 382421, Gujarat, India.
Tel: (079) 39830100, **Email:** info@dadabhagwan.org

Ahmedabad : **Dada Darshan**, 5, Mamtapark Society, B/h. Navgujarat College, Usmanpura, Ahmedabad- 14. **Tel.:** (079) 27540408

Rajkot : **Trimandir**, Ahmedabad-Rajkot Highway, Nr. Targhadiya Cross Road, Maliyasan Village, Rajkot. **Cell:** 9274111393

Bhuj : **Trimandir**, Behind Hill Garden, Airport Road, Near Sahyognagar, Bhuj (Kutch). **Tel.:** (02832) 290123

Godhra : **Trimandir**, Village-Bhamaiya, Opp. FCI Godown, Godhra, Dist.-Panchmahal. **Tel.:** (02672) 262300

Morbi : **Trimandir**, Village-Jepur, Morbi-Navlakhi Road, Morbi, Dist.-Rajkot. **Tel.:** (02822) 297097

Surendranagar: **Trimandir**, Nr. Lok Vidyalaya, Surendranagar-Rajkot Highway, Muli Road, Surendranagar. **Tel.:** 9737048322

Amreli : **Trimandir**, Liliya road bypass chokadi, Kharawadi, Dist - Amreli. **Tel.:** 9924344460

Vadodara : **Dada Mandir**, 17, Mama ni Pol (Street), Opp. Raopura Police Station, Salatvada, Vadodara. **Cell.:** 9924343335

Mumbai : Dada Bhagwan Parivar, **Cell.:** 9323528901

Bangalore : Dada Bhagwan Parivar, **Cell.:** 9590979099

U.S.A.: **Dada Bhagwan Vignan Institute:**
100, SW Redbud Lane, Topeka, Kansas 66606
Tel.: +1 877-505-DADA (3232),
Email: info@us.dadabhagwan.org

U.K.: **Dada Darshan (UK)**, Unit 2, Columbus House, Stonefield Way, Ruislip, HA4 0JA
Tel. :+44 330-111-DADA (3232),
Email : info@uk.dadabhagwan.org

Kenya : +254 722 722 063   **Singapore** : +65 81129229

Australia : +61 421127947   **New Zealand** : +64 21 0376434

UAE : +971 557316937   **Germany** : +49 700 32327474

www.dadabhagwan.org, www.dadashri.org